Praise for *Pittsburg*

MW00514399

I have often said that there is a "global" quality to music that helps bring people together. I am grateful that as conductor of the Pittsburgh Symphony Pops Orchestra I can be a part of that process. On the same note, I believe this book will bring the people of our city together in a meaningful way. Great job, Joanne, and thank you for including the Symphony as one of your reasons to love Pittsburgh!
—Marvin Hamlisch, Principal Pops Conductor

I am not surprised that the city as a whole, and its people and places, are so fabulous. There is a great innovative spirit here, both scientifically and culturally. *Pittsburgh Will Steel Your Heart* touches on many of the city's greatest achievements—every citizen should read it with a sense of pride.
—Dr. Tom Starzl, Distinguished Service Professor of Surgery at the University of Pittsburgh Medical Center

Thanks to Joanne, the countdown to our region's 250th anniversary has truly begun. She's found 250 reasons to love Pittsburgh. Give a copy to your favorite Pittsburgher as an early "birthday present." And just imagine what you can do here!
—Bill Flanagan, Executive Vice President, Corporate Relations, Allegheny Conference on Community Development

As the head team physician for the Pitt Athletic Department, I have had a lot of interaction over the years with team members and their fans. It is always great to see how much people love their team and how often that love spills over to the city itself. Clearly Joanne is one of those fans who just can't get enough of Pittsburgh. Her book is a timely reminder of why we love our city so much.

—Dr. Freddie H. Fu, World-renowned Orthopaedic Surgeon at the University of Pittsburgh Medical Center

Cool ones! Blow your horn if you love this book! I expect to hear honking from every car on the Parkway. What a great way to celebrate the city's unique history, culture, and all that groovy food. Everyone in Pittsburgh should read Joanne Sujansky's fun, fantastic book!

—The Legend Porky Chedwick, Former Pittsburgh Radio D.J.

PITTSBURGH WILL STEEL YOUR HEART

250 Reasons to Love Pittsburgh

A fun & fascinating look at what makes Pittsburgh unique . . . in honor of our 250th birthday in 2008.

Joanne G. Sujansky, Ph.D.
Certified Speaking Professional

Copyright © 2006 Joanne G. Sujansky, Ph.D., Certified Speaking Professional

ISBN-10: 0-9748299-1-9

ISBN-13: 978-0-9748299-1-3

Library of Congress Control Number: 2006935022

Pittsburgh Professional Publishing
306 Marberry Drive
Pittsburgh, PA 15215
412-784-8811

Book Design and Production: Andra Keller, Rocks-DeHart Public Relations

Photos on pages 19, 22, 36, 45, 68, and 87—Copyright, Pittsburgh Post-Gazette, 2006, All rights reserved. Reprinted with permission.

All rights reserved. Printed in the United States. No part of this book may be used or reproduced in any form or by any means, or stored in a database or retrieval system without the prior written permission of the publisher, except in the case of brief quotations embodied in critical articles or reviews. Making copies of any part of this book for any purpose other than your own personal use is a violation of United States copyright laws. Entering any of the contents into a computer for mailing list or database purposes is strictly prohibited unless written authorization is obtained from the publisher.

Dear Pittsburgh Lover:

I *can* call you that, can't I? If you're not in love with our great city right now, you certainly will be by the time you read this book!

Pittsburgh Will Steel Your Heart is a compilation of short, simple "word snapshots" of what makes Pittsburgh, well, *Pittsburgh*. I put this book together with the help of a diverse group of friends, business associates, and fellow citizens who share my sentiments about our fabulous city.

In case you haven't figured it out yet, I LOVE PITTSBURGH! I speak so often about our great city that my clients have fondly referred to me as the Ambassador of Pittsburgh.

This city is where I live, work, and play and—hopefully—where I will eventually (when I'm 90, perhaps) retire. There is a beauty, a vibrant spirit, and a unique culture in Pittsburgh that I have not found anywhere else on the globe.

Why did I write this book? Well, most obviously, I wanted to honor our city on its 250th birthday in 2008. But beyond that, I wanted to share the good news about Pittsburgh to the best of my ability—with businesses, with tourists, and with future and current residents.

This fun book, along with the equally "Pittsburgh-centric" website www.pittsburghwillsteelyourheart.com, represents my very own grassroots campaign to tell the world about our great city. I hope you will join in.

First, share this book with friends. You can let them borrow your copy or, better still, you can buy a few extras to hand out. (They make great gifts!)

Second, please visit my website often. Not only can you get more copies of this book there, you can order some other Pittsburgh items, and you can tell us what *you* love about Pittsburgh.

If you would like to get involved in my Pittsburgh promotion, I will be glad to help you brainstorm ways that you, your company, or your civic organization can join in the excitement. You may already have some ideas of your own . . . and I would love to hear them.

I am excited about helping Pittsburgh "steel" as many hearts as possible. Join me, won't you? An entire city will thank you for your efforts.

Joanne G. Sujansky, Ph.D., Certified Speaking Professional
Founder & CEO, KEYGroup®
Pittsburgh, Pennsylvania

1

Once we were the world leader in steel production. Today we're well on our way to being the world leader in medicine, high-tech, and education.

2

Beautiful churches, big and small, featuring stained glass and steeples of all types, grace almost every neighborhood.

3

Seeing the kayakers and rowing teams
on all of our rivers. And we are
home to Three Rivers Rowing Association.

4

Pittsburgh has a good sense of its history.

5

The Carnegie Science Center, one of the top five
science museums in the nation.

6

The Enrico Biscotti Company in the
Strip District makes the best biscotti
you will ever taste.

7

The hottest spot in town is the Pittsburgh Glass
Center at Penn and Friendship Avenues, where
ovens for making glass can reach
almost 2,400 degrees.

"I Remember Isaly's"

Isaly's ORIGINAL

CHIPPED CHOPPED HAM

HOMETOWN FAVORITE FOR GENERATION

8

Isaly's chipped chopped ham is a refrigerator
staff in most households.

9

People still ask where you went to high school.

10

Google opening an office here because it could not get talented people to move to its offices in California.

11

Most people know the Strip District for its ethnic grocery stores and delicious produce—and yet few realize it has also been home to a saint. St. John Neumann served as pastor of St. Philomena, Strip District, from 1844 to 1847 and was canonized a saint in 1977.

12

In 2006, *Esquire* magazine rated Pittsburgh as
best among "Cities that Rock" in
the United States.

13

We're the only place in the world to
offer a Ph.D. in robotics
(Carnegie Mellon University).

14

Streets that run neither parallel
nor perpendicular.

15

We've used and revised the land. In fact, we rank second in green-certified space among cities in the nation and we are home to the world's largest "green" building, the David H. Lawrence Convention Center.

16

Lots of "mom and pop" pizza parlors making delectable pizza with a wide array of toppings.

17

The Steel Curtain.

18

Thanks to the clear water of the Allegheny River,
you can actually catch big fish downtown.

19

The word "yunz"—a true Pittsburgh original.

20

Director George Romero attended Carnegie Mellon University and is most well known for *Night of the Living Dead*, filmed here in Pittsburgh.

21

George Washington slept here!

22

America's first and most dramatic "urban renewal" in the '50s and '60s transformed our downtown area.

23

Senator John Heinz Pittsburgh Regional History Center, Pennsylvania's largest history museum. It also includes the Western PA Sports Museum and a Special Collections gallery.

24

The horrible disease of polio was itself crippled by the research of Dr. Jonas Salk at the University of Pittsburgh.

25

There are 89 trade and technical schools
in the region, opening opportunities to those
who do not attend college.

26

We're home to the National Aviary—the
only bird zoo in the nation.

27

Parkway East traffic backed up to
the Squirrel Hill Tunnel.

28

We have hundreds of miles of walking, hiking,
and bike trails along waterfronts and
through wooded hillsides.

29

The United States' first commercially successful plate glass maker was the Pittsburgh Plate Glass Company (PPG), founded in Creighton in 1883. It has paid its shareholders uninterrupted dividends since 1899.

30

The right-field wall at PNC Park is 21 feet high in honor of legendary Pirates right fielder Roberto Clemente, who wore number 21.

31

Pittsburgh has become a high-tech center. We specialize in Internet security and other 21st century themes.

32
You can still go to drive-in theaters.

33
Spring in Pittsburgh is a spectacular
explosion of greenery and blossoms
that is especially vibrant after a cold winter.

34
Musical legend Perry Como was born
in Canonsburg in 1912.

35

The Pittsburgh region is home to 446 bridges,
the most of any city in the world.

36

The central rotunda, capped by
a stained-glass dome, in the landmark
Union Trust Building, now Mellon One.

37

You can "redd up" your room.

38

Two hundred fifty thousand people showed up
for the Super Bowl XL Victory Parade held
February 7, 2006. That's right . . . a quarter
of a million people!

39

It's just a few miles to Moon and Mars.

40

People say "gum band" for "rubber band."

41

The Immaculate Reception.

42

Pittsburgh has been a spawn of movie talent,
from John Hodiak to Michael Keaton.

43

Pittsburghers are really caffeinated! We purchase
more coffee—3.4 pounds per capita—than any
other major American city.

44

"Dinosaurs in Their World" exhibit at the Carnegie
Museum of Natural History, the most exciting and
interesting dinosaur exhibit in the world.

45

Almost thirty thousand visitors a year tour the Cathedral of Learning's twenty-six nationality classrooms, which display the diverse ethnic heritage of Pittsburgh. The Cathedral of Learning is the only skyscraper university building in the United States.

46

Gertrude Stein, American expatriate, writer, and confidant of Ernest Hemingway, was born in Pittsburgh in 1874. When speaking about her hometown once, someone asked her, "What's it like there?" She famously replied, "There is no there, there." Fortunately she was speaking about Oakland, California, where she later grew up.

47

The area is abundant in golf courses.
We rank first (or nearly first)
in number of places to play per person.

48

Two degrees of separation instead of six.

49

Our broadcast celebrities are easy to talk
with and relate to.

50

Hanging over the railing of the Schenley Park
Bridge to view the amazing
Panther Hollow Lake.

51

Churches that sell homemade gnocchi.

52

The downtown skyline at night is
spectacular—especially during
"Light Up Night"
and Monday Night Football.

53

In its annual "World in 2006" issue,
The Economist magazine rated 127 cities from around the
world as best places for business travel. Pittsburgh ranked #11.

54

On June 6, 1949, a small thirteen-seat drive-in restaurant
called Eat 'n Park opened in Pittsburgh's South Hills. Ten
carhops served the throng of customers that flowed along
Saw Mill Run Boulevard. The restaurant had to close down
after six hours because so many cars tried to pull into the
parking lot that a huge traffic jam ensued. Needless to say,
Eat 'n Park was able to regroup and re-open . . . and now it's
famous for the happy face sugar cookie, "Smiley."

55

You can dance to polka music, the Electric Slide,
and the Chicken Song at weddings.

56

Sunset at the golden triangle
when the golden bridges glow.

57

The Thunderbolt rollercoaster at Kennywood
Park was named the number one rollercoaster in
the world by the National Amusement Park
Historical Association.

58

In 1886, The Pittsburgh Brewing Company—makers of Iron City
Beer—became so successful that it had to move its operation from
its original facilities on 17th Street to a four-story brick building
on Liberty and 34th Street. The company's headquarters
remain there today.

59

The Three Rivers Arts Festival, an awesome
consortium of world-renowned
artists, attracts thousands despite
the rain showers in June.

60

We have five professional sports teams.

61

The Christmas tree and skating rink at PPG Place.

62

Martha Graham, a pioneer in modern dance,
was born in Pittsburgh in 1894.

63

People may leave but
they come back.

64

Our wonderful ethnic
neighborhoods.

65

Pittsburgh is where Elizabeth Jane Cochrane, a.k.a. "Nellie Bly," started her journalism career in 1885. She was hired by the editor of *The Pittsburgh Dispatch* after writing a letter of protest about a sexist article that appeared in the paper. (Cool sidenote: She got her pseudonym from a song by Pittsburgh native Stephen Foster.)

66

World-renowned maestros.

67

The visionaries who have made their homes
here—from Dr. Jonas Salk to Dr. Starzl.

68

Benefactors such as Scaife, Mellon,
and Frick are household names.

69

From the Pittsburgh Symphony to the
Pittsburgh Ballet, the cultural district
is alive at night.

70

Christina Aguilera, a famous pop singer,
graduated from North Allegheny High School.

71

The Pittsburgh accent—nothing like
it anywhere else n'at. Here people
say "dahntahn" for "downtown."

72

Doo Wop groups like Johnny Angel and the Halos and Jimmy Beaumont and the Skyliners.

73

Shirley Jones, the mom on *The Partridge Family*, was born in Charleroi in 1934. After graduating high school, she entered the Miss Pittsburgh Pageant and won. She still visits our city yearly for family reunions.

74

Listening to accordion music while you wait for your fish at Wholey's.

75

In Pittsburgh so many things are within walking distance. You can walk the downtown area without doing a marathon—and without getting mugged.

76

Pittsburgh is the eighteenth most educated city in the U.S., with 33.6 percent of the population having a college degree or higher. There are forty-four colleges and universities in the Pittsburgh area.

77
We're the home of
Sarris chocolates.

78
The Andy Warhol (born Andrew Warhola in
Pittsburgh) Museum, a one-of-a-kind gallery
devoted to American pop culture.

79

There's a niche for everyone. Whatever pleases
your palate, Pittsburgh has that flavor.

80

The Steelers were called the Pirates for seven
seasons. Founder Art Rooney renamed his team
the Steelers in 1940.

81

The airport is very efficient and convenient
and has a T-Rex that stands 15 feet high
greeting you when you arrive.

82

Walking across the 6th Street Bridge for
a Pirates game. And fireworks at
the end of the game.

83

The way the downtown jumps out at you when
you first come out of the Fort Pitt tunnel.

84

Mellon Financial Corporation was the first major bank in the
U.S. to introduce computers into the banking business.
Installed in the early 1950s, IBM model 650 weighed
two-and-a-half tons, took up a large room, and offered about
the same computing power as today's pocket calculators.

85

People look forward to, celebrate, and decorate for all holidays—even Groundhog Day.

86

All the unique stairways from street to street leading to homes perched on the various hills in the city.

87

"Meet me under the clock"—the Kaufmann's clock, of course. (Now owned by Macy's.)

88

An announcement about a possible cure for arthritis was made in a medical lab by people wearing Steelers jerseys.

89

Driving our narrow roads keeps you on your toes.

90

Mary Cassatt, one of the leading members of the impressionist movement, was born in Pittsburgh in 1845.

91

People nationwide doing business with your company simply because "they grew up in Pittsburgh."

92

We actually have four distinct seasons.
(Variety is good!)

93

People are glad to spend 10 minutes (or more)
to try to give directions to strangers
who stop them on a corner.

94

You can still order from a drive-in carhop, Jerry's
Curb Service, in Beaver County, a mere
30-minute drive from downtown Pittsburgh.

95

With all the wild turkeys, skunks, deer, raccoons, and other creatures, your backyard might as well be a petting zoo.

96

We still have roller rinks and kids
still like going to them.

97

Station Square: the place to go for dining, entertainment,
shopping, and celebrating after ball games. You can park at
Station Square and ride one of the Gateway Clipper boats
before and after the Steelers, Pirates, and Panthers games.

98

Our fantastic state-of-the-art medical care and
our variety of world-renowned hospitals.

99

USA Today Weekend Magazine named the nighttime view from Mt. Washington the second most beautiful place in America in 2003.

100

Oldies music and school reunions let you revisit your roots—and roots matter in Pittsburgh.

101

Reserving the parking spot in front of your house with a chair.

102

Two of the greatest baseball teams in the former Negro League, the Crawfords and the Homestead Grays, were sponsored here, producing greats like Satchel Paige and Josh Gibson.

103

The first arena with a retractable roof dome.

104

The reflections of the lights on the three rivers.

105

All of our eccentric heroes: Former Mayor Sophie Masloff, Steeler Commentator Myron Cope, and The Legend, Porky Chedwick.

106

The Allegheny County Jail in Pittsburgh was the site of Mrs. Soffel's legendary crime—her home on the top of Mt. Washington is now a fine eatery.

107

Lawrence Welk's bubble machine was
invented here.

108

When U.S. Steel was founded in Pittsburgh in
1901, it was the largest business enterprise ever
launched. It remains the largest integrated steel
producer in the country today.

109

The Vogues from Turtle Creek—a great singing
group of the '60s and '70s.

110

The riverboats, especially the Gateway Clipper Fleet.

111

The place where two rivers come together to
make a new river, the Ohio.
(No other city has a triangle like ours!)

112

Pittsburghers will typically give you the shirts off their backs
(provided they're not Steelers, Penguins, or Pirates shirts).

113
Pierogies are a food group.

114

The Just Ducky tours of Pittsburgh's roads and rivers.

115

You never know what to expect when you're in a strange part of town: what's over the next hill, around the bend, or one street over.

116

Founded in Pittsburgh in 1888, the Aluminum Company of America (Alcoa) is the world's leading producer of aluminum and was named one of the top three most sustainable corporations in the world at the World Economic Forum.

117
School closings are
major news events
in January and Februar

118
Jeff Goldblum, whose catchphrase "Must go faster!"
has been used in at least 11 of his films,
is a Pittsburgh native.

119

We have lots of people who volunteer.

120

Shanice, a Grammy-nominated American R&B singer, is a native of Pittsburgh. Interesting factoid: at the age of nine, she starred in a Kentucky Fried Chicken commercial with Ella Fitzgerald.

121

Real estate is reasonable.

122

The Steelers in the red zone at Heinz Field. It's even more fun because we're the home of Heinz ketchup.

123

Pittsburgh has many activities and programs for the elderly.

124

The Big Mac® was invented at a McDonald's franchise in Uniontown in 1967.

125

Rachel Carson, the internationally renowned conservationist, was born in Springdale in 1907.

126

Fabulous parks.

127

David McCullough, a two-time winner of the Pulitzer Prize, graduated from Shady Side Academy. Best known for his books, which include *The Johnstown Flood*, he has been referred to as "a master of the art of narrative history."

128

The *Pierogies Race* at PNC Park. No matter how many times you see it, it is still funny.

129

You can watch Peregrine Falcons that live downtown on a webcam.

130

The green of the trees on the hillsides along the rivers in the spring. The red and gold of those same trees in the fall.

131

Barbara Feldon of *Get Smart* fame is a graduate
of Bethel Park High School.

132

The Pitt News, a financially independent
newspaper written and managed by students at
the University of Pittsburgh, soon will be
celebrating its 100th year of publication.

133

You can get there from here: Pittsburgh is located
halfway between New York City and Chicago and is
within a two hour flight or a day's drive of more
than 70 percent of the U.S. population.

134

The International Poetry Forum was founded in 1966 by
Duquesne University's Dr. Samuel Hazo and attracts
an international gathering of poets, writers,
and artists to the city every year.

135

Dennis Miller, a famous comedian, is a product
of the Pittsburgh Public Schools.

136

When you have a block party, you actually
know your neighbors.

137

You can still find a high school student happy to cut your lawn. And kids still want to babysit.

138

You can't get a table anywhere on a Friday night without a 45-minute wait. (Why is this a positive? It proves we have great restaurants and a booming economy!)

139

Italian is the predominant ethnic food of choice.

140

There is nothing like a high school football
game in October…priceless.

141

Pittsburgh: where the slightest hint of snow sends
people running to the grocery store
to stock up on bread and milk.

142

People still like to make crafts.

143

North Hills, South Hills, Penn Hills, Polish Hill, Squirrel Hill, and the Hill District—get the picture?

144

In 1987, the founder of 84 Lumber Company, Joseph A. Hardy III, purchased Nemacolin Woodlands Resort at an auction. He has turned it into a world-class resort that has one of the most distinguished art collections in the area.

145
Being so close to a top ski resort: Seven Springs.

146
Forcing the kids to go on a tour of Frank Lloyd Wright's Fallingwater and Kentuck Knob and them ending up loving

147

Wonderful hideaway neighborhoods like
Chatham Village on Mt. Washington.

148

Pittsburgh jumped to the nation's third-best
mid-sized arts city in a readers' poll released
in 2006 by *AmericanStyle* magazine.

149

Festivals celebrating the various nationalities of
Pittsburghers...Italian, Irish, Serbian and
Greek, to name a few.

150

Fantastic and fun public pools where your stuff is safe
while you are in the water.

151

The number of parents who volunteer as
Little League coaches.

152

Everyone eats ham at Easter. (Pick yours up early or you will be standing in line for 45 minutes.)

153

You get to build a snowman at least once or twice a year.

154

Home to music legends Henry Mancini, George Benson, Billy Eckstine, and Lena Horne.

155
Bob Hope proposed to his wife, Delores, in
Pittsburgh's William Penn Hotel, a historic landmark.
Gee...Bob Hope was born before it was built!

156
Outdoor ice rinks.

157
People are not flashy with their money.

158

The Pittsburgh Debs, a women's open softball team, won
the 1970 & 1971 USSA World Championship. Susan Stead
was the 1970 MVP and Jeri Riedel was the 1971 MVP.

159

We have the largest nativity scene—a replica
of the one in Bethlehem.

160

Our airport has the best shopping of any airport in the country.

161

December brings the Christmas tree on the old Horne's building.

162

We've been the temporary home to at least three saints: John Neumann, Francis Seelos, and Katharine Drexel.

163

Mr. Yuk, a green "yucky" face label warning children not to ingest poisonous substances, was conceived in 1971 at the Poison Center at the Children's Hospital of Pittsburgh. Mr. Yuk replaces the traditional skull-and-crossbones label, which research proves does little to deter children because they equate the Jolly Roger with pirates and excitement.

164

"Going out" means dinner and a movie.

165

Charlie Daniels hails Pittsburgh Steelers fans in
the song *In America*.

166

America's first television station,
KDKA, began here in 1920.

167

Robert Morris University is named after a man
who helped finance the Revolutionary War and
who was one of three individuals who signed The
Declaration of Independence, The Bill of Rights,
and The Constitution.

168

The history. Fort Pitt was a central location in
the French and Indian War.

169

Julie Benz, who played Darla in the television
series *Angel*, was born in Pittsburgh in 1972.

170

The Duquesne and Monongahela Inclines.

171

No matter where you go in Pittsburgh, you're likely to run into someone you know.

172

Tugboats and barges on the river.

173

Gardening is not a lost art.

174

Everyone remembers 1979 as the year the Pirates won the World Series and the Steelers won the Super Bowl.

175

Pittsburgh drivers are ultra-polite and will insist that you go first!

176

Pittsburgh is a great place to network and do business. Visit www.pittsburghwillsteelyourheart.com to get started.

177

You can play a game of bingo in a multitude of neighborhood churches. Bingo was invented by Pittsburgher Hugh Ward.

178

The Smithfield Street Bridge, built in 1818, was originally a covered wooden span. It opened as the region's first river bridge.

179

Pittsburgh is quite sophisticated in an unassuming way.

180

Schools are closed the Monday after Thanksgiving for the first day of deer (hunting) season.

181

Mystery writer Mary Roberts Rinehart was born here. She wrote 52 murder mysteries and coined the phrase, "The butler did it!"

182

The average commute to work in
Pittsburgh is less than the national average.

183

Eating a hotdog at PNC Park on opening day.

184

Pittsburghers are strangely preoccupied with the weather,
which gives us plenty to talk about.

185

For a fun Saturday, take the trolley downtown.

186

It's a great place to raise a family.

187

The fact that the home plate from
Forbes Field is in Forbes Quadrangle at the
University of Pittsburgh.

188

The drive past the river on the Boulevard of the Allies.

189

How Pittsburgh has reinvented
itself over and over.

190

The mystery of the B-25 that crashed into the Allegheny River during WWII and was never found.

191

People use the word "nebby" to mean "nosey."

192

It's the only city where 6th Street and 6th Avenue run parallel to each other.

193

There is nothing like sinking your teeth into a Primanti Brothers sandwich.

194

When someone makes a list of the "most livable cities in America," we're *always* near the top.

195

Popular *sports only* talk radio shows.

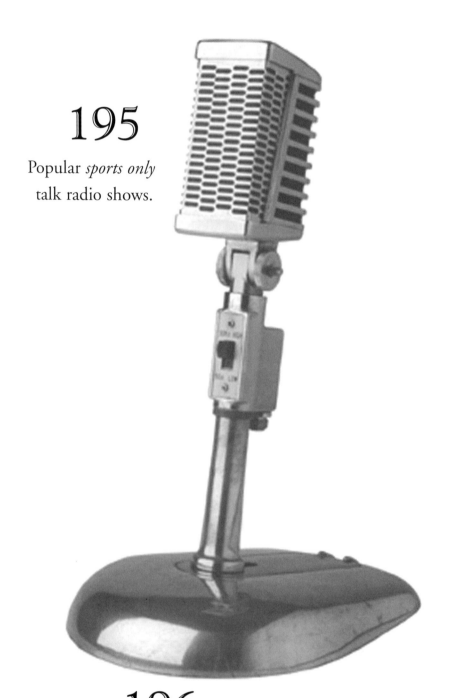

196

Young people respect (and talk to) older people here.

197

Pittsburgh has more restaurants and eateries per capita than any large city in America.

198

Bookstores galore. (Independents, too!)

199

It's fun to change clothing
with the frequent change of weather!

200

Our historic architecture reaches all the
way back to the 18th century!

201

Pittsburgh is the second busiest inland port in America.

202

The abundance of trees (the Squirrel Hill Tunnel
looks like it comes out of a forest).

203

Everybody in Pittsburgh forgets how to drive in
the snow during the first snowfall of the season.

204

Free concerts at Hartwood Acres, the Point,
and South Park every summer.

205

The stellar Phipps Conservatory.

206

Pittsburghers and residents from throughout the
region throng downtown for events like
"Light Up Night" and "First Night."

207
The air shows at Allegheny County Airport.

208
Pittsburgh is home to not one, but <u>two</u> fully restored, historically rich, world-class concert halls.

209

Point State Park's fountain sprays 6,000 gallons
of water per minute.

210

Game 4 of the 1971 World Series, played at Three Rivers
Stadium, was the first World Series night game ever played.

211

The outdoor concert pavilion in Burgettstown.

212

"Le Magnifique" and "Super Mario" are affectionately respectful nicknames for hockey icon Mario Lemieux, who played for the Pittsburgh Penguins for 17 seasons (from 1984 to 2006). He will forever be regarded as one of the greatest hockey players in the NHL.

213

Oakland is abuzz with college kids.

214

Memories of smartly dressed women who used to wear their white gloves and hats to shop downtown.

215
Nightlife on the Southside and in the Strip.

216
Twists and turns on Mt. Washington that make
San Francisco look tame.

217
Fries on salads…and in sandwiches…and on the side.

218

The rotunda and stairway of the Grand Concourse, originally the Pittsburgh & Lake Erie train station built in 1898, in Station Square.

219

We're no longer the "Smoky City."

220

People give directions based on "what used to be there."

221

"One-Shot" Teenie Harris—a renowned African American photographer who captured the essence of the Black community in Pittsburgh.

222
The world's first Ferris Wheel was created by Pittsburgh bridge builder George W. Ferris in 1893.

223
Myron Cope's Terrible Towel proceeds have helped raise almost $1.1 million for the Allegheny Valley School, which provides care for more than 900 people with mental retardation and physical disabilities.

224
Libraries funded by Andrew Carnegie, who is said to have given rise to modern philanthropy. After playwright August Wilson—who grew up in the Hill District—dropped out of high school, he continued his education on his own at the Carnegie Library in Oakland.

225

The first movie theater in the United States, named the "Nickelodeon" because admission was a nickel, was opened in Pittsburgh in 1905.

226

We fought to retain the "h" at the end of Pittsburgh, even after an edict from the U.S. Board of Geographic Names ordered it to be removed.

227

The first Ice Capades performance
was in Pittsburgh in 1940.

228

Natives from mill towns may fondly remember the
old days when plant workers walked home with their
lunch buckets and thermoses.

229

In 1979, decades before online shopping became a reality, Federated Investors, Inc., headquartered in Liberty Center, downtown Pittsburgh, invented EDGE (Electronic Data Gathering Extension), the mutual fund industry's first online order-entry system for purchasing and redeeming fund shares. Today, EDGEnet provides Internet account access.

230

There is no need to plant bulbs in the fall as the chipmunks eat them before they can bloom.

231

You can take a backyard composting class and receive a free compost bin from the City of Pittsburgh.

232

During the Civil War, Pittsburgh was one of the major suppliers of cannons and heavy guns to the Union cause. The cannons that manned the *USS Monitor* were made in Pittsburgh.

233

We have a lot of "mature" workers—Pittsburghers don't like to retire.

234

Famous former Pittsburgh Steeler Franco Harris has his own line of "healthy" donuts.

235

Quaint shopping in Shadyside and Sewickley.

236

The almond torte at Prantl's Bakery in Shadyside—
one bite and you'll crave it forever!

237

The Klondike Bar was invented by the Isaly
family (of Isaly's chipped chopped ham fame).

238

We are close to Amish country.

239

Gene Kelly perfected his skills dancing between
the raindrops in his native Pittsburgh.

240

Willa Cather, author of the classic American novel *My
Antonia* worked for the *Pittsburgh Post-Gazette* early in her
career and set one of her short stories in Pittsburgh.

241

The Jeep was invented in Pittsburgh (by Willys
Mfg. Company in Butler in the late 1930s).

242

America's most renowned bridge builder—John A. Roebling, who built the Brooklyn Bridge—perfected his engineering techniques in and around Pittsburgh in the 1840s to 1860s.

243

Only city where all sports teams have the same colors.

244

In 1940 the residents of Pittsburgh offered a $1 million reward for the capture of Adolph Hitler.

245

The first steamboat to ply western waters, the *New Orleans*, was built in Pittsburgh in 1911.

246

Pulitzer Prize-winning playwrights George S. Kaufman (1889) and Marc Connelly (1890) were both born in Pittsburgh.

247

At Candy-Rama, a favorite shop for young and
old alike, you'll find treats from your past,
including "old style" boxes that sold for 10 cents,
to conjure up fabulous memories.

248

The first community-financed television station in the
country was Pittsburgh's WQED.

249

America's landmark children's show,
Mister Rogers' Neighborhood, was produced
in Pittsburgh from 1967 to 2001.

250

It's home.

Now I would like to hear your reasons.

Why do you love Pittsburgh?

Visit www.pittsburghwillsteelyourheart.com

and click on the "tell me what you love" tab.